BASEBALL LEGENDS

Hank Aaron
Grover Cleveland Alexander
Ernie Banks
Johnny Bench
Yogi Berra
Roy Campanella
Roberto Clemente
Ty Cobb
Dizzy Dean
Joe DiMaggio
Bob Feller
Jimmie Foxx
Lou Gehrig
Bob Gibson
Rogers Hornsby
Reggie Jackson
Shoeless Joe Jackson
Walter Johnson
Sandy Koufax
Mickey Mantle
Christy Mathewson
Willie Mays
Stan Musial
Satchel Paige
Brooks Robinson
Frank Robinson
Jackie Robinson
Pete Rose
Babe Ruth
Nolan Ryan
Mike Schmidt
Tom Seaver
Duke Snider
Warren Spahn
Willie Stargell
Casey Stengel
Honus Wagner
Ted Williams
Carl Yastrzemski
Cy Young

NEWFIELD
PUBLICATIONS

CHRISTY MATHEWSON

Norman L. Macht

Introduction by
Jim Murray

Senior Consultant
Earl Weaver

CHELSEA HOUSE PUBLISHERS
New York • Philadelphia

The author wishes to thank Kate Lambert and her 1990 fifth-grade class at Monroe-Maltby Elementary School, Snohomish, Washington, for their help in this and other volumes in this series.

Published by arrangement with Chelsea House Publishers. Newfield Publications is a federally registered trademark of Newfield Publications, Inc.

Produced by James Charlton Associates New York, New York.

Designed by Hudson Studio Ossining, New York.

Typesetting by LinoGraphics New York, New York.

Picture research by Carolann Hawkins Cover illustration by Dan O'Leary

Library of Congress Cataloging-in-Publication Data

Macht, Norman L. (Norman Lee), 1929-
    Christy Mathewson / Norman Macht; introduction by Jim Murray; senior consultant, Earl Weaver.
    p. cm.—(Baseball legends)
Includes bibliographical references and index.
    Summary: Follows the life and career of Baseball Hall of Fame pitcher Christy Mathewson.
    ISBN 0-7910-1182-8.—ISBN 0-7910-1266-9 (pbk.)
    1. Mathewson, Christy, 1880-1925—Juvenile literature.
    2. Baseball players—United States—Biography—Juvenile literature.
    [1. Mathewson, Christy, 1880 1925. 2. Baseball players.]
    I. Series.
GV865.M37M33 1991
92—dc20
[796.357'092]   90-41515
[B]   CIP
                                                       AC

CONTENTS

WHAT MAKES A STAR

Jim Murray

No one has ever been able to explain to me the mysterious alchemy that makes one man a .350 hitter and another player, more or less identical in physical makeup, hard put to hit .200. You look at an Al Kaline, who played with the Detroit Tigers from 1953 to 1974. He was pale, stringy, almost poetic-looking. He always seemed to be struggling against a bad case of mononucleosis. But with a bat in his hands, he was King Kong. During his career, he hit 399 home runs, rapped out 3,007 hits, and compiled a .297 batting average.

Form isn't the reason. The first time anybody saw Roberto Clemente step into the batter's box for the Pittsburgh Pirates, the best guess was that Clemente would be back in Double A ball in a week. He had one foot in the bucket and held his bat at an awkward angle—he looked as though he couldn't hit an outside pitch. A lot of other ballplayers may have had a better-looking stance. Yet they never led the National League in hitting in four different years, the way Clemente did.

Not cvcry ballplaycr is born with the ability to hit a curveball. Nor is exceptional hand-eye coordination the key to heavy hitting. Big-league locker rooms are filled with players who have all the attributes, save one: discipline. Every baseball man can tell you a story about a pitcher who throws a ball faster than anyone has ever seen but who has no control on or *off* the field.

The Hall of Fame is full of people who transformed themselves into great ballplayers by working at the sport, by studying the game, and making sacrifices. They're overachievers—and winners. If you want to find them, just watch the World Series. Or simply read about New York Yankee great Lou Gehrig; Ted Williams, "the Splendid Splinter" of the Boston Red Sox; or the Dodgers' strikeout king Sandy Koufax.

A pitcher *should* be able to win a lot of ballgames with a 98-miles-per-hour fastball. But what about the pitcher who wins 20 games a year with a fastball so slow that you can catch it with your teeth? Bob Feller of the Cleveland Indians got into the Hall of Fame with a blazing fastball that glowed in the dark. National League star Grover Cleveland Alexander got there with a pitch that took considerably longer to reach the plate; but when it did arrive, the pitch was exactly where Alexander wanted it to be—and the last place the batter expected it to be.

There are probably more players with exceptional ability who didn't make it to the major leagues than there are who did. A number of great hitters, bored with fielding practice, had to be dropped from their team because their home-run production didn't make up for their lapses in the field. And then there are players like Brooks Robinson of the Baltimore Orioles, who made himself into a human vacuum cleaner at third base because he knew that working hard to become an expert fielder would win him a job in the big leagues.

A star is not something that flashes through the sky. That's a comet. Or a meteor. A star is something you can steer ships by. It stays in place and gives off a steady glow; it is fixed, permanent. A star works at being a star.

And that's how you tell a star in baseball. He shows up night after night and takes pride in how brightly he shines. He's Willie Mays running so hard his hat keeps falling off; Ty Cobb sliding to stretch a single into a double; Lou Gehrig, after being fooled in his first two at-bats, belting the next pitch off the light tower because he's taken the time to study the pitcher. Stars never take themselves for granted. That's why they're stars.

1
LOSING A BIG ONE

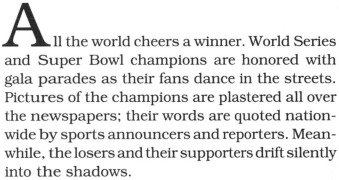

All the world cheers a winner. World Series and Super Bowl champions are honored with gala parades as their fans dance in the streets. Pictures of the champions are plastered all over the newspapers; their words are quoted nationwide by sports announcers and reporters. Meanwhile, the losers and their supporters drift silently into the shadows.

Once in a great while, however, a gallant loser is hailed even more than his conquerors. Because of his popularity, his character, and the courageous battle he has fought, his place in the hearts of those who have watched him becomes even greater in defeat. Even his foes stand and cheer him.

Such a man was Christy Mathewson, one of the noblest sports heroes America has ever

Before the start of game 1 of the 1912 World Series, (left to right) Giants coach Wilbert Robinson, manager John McGraw, and Christy Mathewson watch batting practice. After McGraw accused Robinson of missing a coaching sign in the 1913 World Series, the popular coach left to manage the Brooklyn Dodgers, and the two became bitter rivals.

known. He was a tall, broad-shouldered, handsome man, with a shock of blond, unruly hair and light-blue eyes. Today, he would be said to have movie-star looks.

When Mathewson strode to the pitcher's mound for the New York Giants on Opening Day of the 1901 baseball season, it was as if a knight from King Arthur's round table had suddenly appeared on earth. During the next 12 years, his pitching records, made with poise and pluck and speed and brains, would earn him the title of one of baseball's all-time greatest pitchers.

Mathewson's feats on the diamond might account for his fame, but they do not explain his popularity. It was his fairness and decency that earned him the love and admiration of the entire nation. His control as a pitcher was matched by his self-control as a person. Using his fine intelligence as much as his strong right arm, he worked constantly to improve and was always eager to learn. Mathewson never quarreled with other players, never disputed an umpire's decision. His honesty was unquestioned; once it actually cost his team a place in the World Series. Throughout his long career, he honored his mother's strong religious beliefs by never playing a game on Sunday. In the words of one teammate, "He looked like he meant well toward the whole world."

But somehow, almost as if to show that no man is entitled to every blessing life has to offer, Christy Mathewson had nothing but bad luck and tough breaks in the biggest games he was called upon to pitch—and, indeed, in the game of life itself.

And so it was on October 9, 1912. Mathewson and the New York Giants had battled the Boston

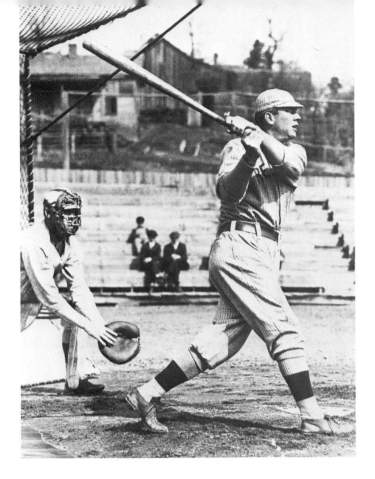

Tris Speaker was the "greatest center fielder of his day;" so reads his Hall of Fame plaque. Speaker played a shallow center field, which enabled him to amass 35 assists in 1909 and again in 1912, still the modern major-league record for centerfielders.

Red Sox to a deciding seventh game in the World Series. The Series should have ended sooner, with a New York victory. In the second game, the 32-year-old Mathewson had outpitched three younger foes for 10 innings, but five errors by his fielders cost him the win. He had to settle for a 6–6 tie when darkness ended the contest. Three days later, an error by the Giants second baseman led to a 2–1 loss even though Matty had retired the last 15 batters in a row.

Now the championship was on the line, and once again manager John McGraw handed the ball to Mathewson. The Giants scored a run in the 3rd, and it remained 1–0 until the Red Sox came to bat in the 7th. It was then that the fates played their first trick of the day on Matty, the man who aspired to perfection. With one out, Boston's player-manager, Jake Stahl, hit a fly ball to short left field. The New York shortstop, leftfielder, and centerfielder converged on it. They all arrived in time to catch the ball, but each one waited for another to take it, and it fell between them. With two men out, a pinch-hitter then doubled in the tying run.

Nobody scored in the 8th or 9th, but in the top of the 10th the Giants went ahead, 2–1. Mathewson then walked to the mound, determined to hold on to the lead and take home the prize. The first batter lifted a high fly ball to centerfielder Fred Snodgrass, who had to move only a few feet to make an easy catch. Incredibly, the ball trickled through his hands for a two-base error. The center fielder then redeemed himself by chasing a long fly ball and making a splendid catch.

Matty, whose control had been perfect in his first two games, walked the next man. That brought Tris Speaker, a .383 hitter, to the plate. Speaker hit a routine pop-up near the first-base coaches' box. Catcher Chief Meyers ran up the baseline as Matty came over from the mound. First baseman Fred Merkle, the closest man to the ball, took a few steps toward it. In the silence that shrouded the ballpark, where Boston's hopes seemed suddenly dashed, Matty called out clearly, "Meyers, Meyers," for the catcher to take it. Then somebody on the Boston bench, hoping to confuse the fielders, yelled, "Matty! Matty!" Merkle could have caught the ball easily, but he backed off to avoid running into the others. Mathewson could have caught it in his bare hand, but he had already called on Meyers. And so Meyers, who had the farthest to run, made a desperate lunge for it. The ball dropped to the ground in foul territory, untouched.

Given another chance, Speaker stood in the batter's box and called to Mathewson, "That's gonna cost you this ball game and the championship." And on the next pitch he lined a clean single that drove in the tying run and moved a man to third. The next batter hit a sacrifice fly to left field, and the winning run scored.

Realizing that even the greatest players sometimes make errors, Mathewson never blamed Snodgrass for dropping the fly ball that started his downfall. "No use hopping on him; he feels three times as bad as any of us," was all Matty said.

Sportswriter Ring Lardner, who was at the game, had a lot more to say about it. "There was seen one of the saddest sights in the history of a sport that is a strange and wonderful mixture of joy and gloom," he wrote. "It was the spectacle of a man, old as baseball players are reckoned, walking from the middle of the field to the New York players' bench with bowed head and drooping shoulders, with tears streaming from his eyes, a man on whom his team's fortune had been staked and lost, and a man who would have proven his clear title to the trust reposed in him if his mates had stood by him in the supreme test. The man was Christy Mathewson.

"Beaten, 3 to 2, by a club he would have conquered if he had been given the support deserved by his wonderful pitching, Matty tonight is greater in the eyes of New York's public than ever before. Even the joy-mad population of Boston confesses that his should have been the victory and his the praise."

LEARNING TO PITCH

Christopher Mathewson was born in Factoryville, Pennsylvania, on August 12, 1880, the first of five children. Set in a valley of corn-fields, pastures, orchards, and streams, the little town was cut off by high hills from the grimy dark air of nearby Scranton, where thousands of coal miners inhaled coal dust deep underground from sunup to dusk. The Mathewson home, set back from a tree-shaded road, was surrounded by an apple orchard, a garden, and a barnyard, where white hens scratched in the dirt. Christy's father, a landowner and developer, had also been born there.

On Sundays, nothing moved in Factoryville unless it was pushed by the wind. The only sounds were the rustle of shades being pulled down in parlors and, weather permitting, the creak of rocking chairs on front porches. The evils of drink were prominently proclaimed, and the names of cities such as New York were seldom uttered without a shudder at the thought of what went on there. Although his mother probably did not extract any formal vows from

Three-year-old Christy shows his pitching form.

Mathewson (left) and a teammate on the Keystone Academy football team.

him, Christy never put on a baseball uniform on Sundays—not even when he became a major leaguer.

By the time he was four, Christy was nagging the older boys to get into their games. They shooed him away, but he would not be daunted. He was determined to prove that he was big enough to join them. Toward that end, he threw

a ball over the roof of the barn to a catcher waiting on the other side. It was a game they called "hailey over." On at least one occasion, his strength proved better than his control. The ball sailed through a neighbor's window, and Christy had to empty his bank to pay for fixing it. "It took Christy a long time to save the dollar the broken window cost," his mother later recalled. "But it taught him a sense of responsibility."

An older cousin helped Christy develop the art of throwing stones. Christy learned quickly that a flat stone, hurled with the flat side parallel to the ground, would turn over before it landed; but if thrown with the flat side at an angle to the ground, it would curve. Since stones were a lot more plentiful and a lot less expensive than baseballs, Christy practiced for hours at a time with them and became an expert at bagging squirrels and other small game. Because of his accuracy, all the boys wanted him on their side in snowball fights.

Christy declared his ambition to be a big-league pitcher when he was only eight. Of course, the National League wasn't so big back then, having been in existence just over 10 years. Reports of games from distant cities were printed in the newspaper, but it was as if they were accounts of mythical contests in faraway places. Baseball, in the real world of Factoryville, meant the town team and its nearby rivals, not a profession where a young man might hope to earn a living.

From grammar school, Christy went to Keystone Academy in the next town, as Factoryville had no high school of its own. He was taller than most of the boys, but at 14 he was the youngest on the school team. He was not much of a hitter

Mathewson, in what is probably a photograph taken for his graduation from Keystone Academy. Christy's younger brother Henry also attended Keystone and later pitched briefly for the New York Giants.

then, and nobody took the time to teach him how to hold the bat correctly.

It was not until the next year that he got his first chance to pitch. Thanks to his practice throwing stones, Christy could throw a variety of curveballs, making a pitch dart sometimes one way and sometimes the other. His most effective toss broke straight down, as if the ball had rolled off the end of a table. They called it a "drop" pitch.

As luck would have it, Factoryville's ace pitcher got sick the day before a big game, while the second-string hurler was out of town. "That Mathewson kid can pitch pretty well," someone told the team captain. The captain checked Christy out and told him to come down to Main Street the next morning, which was Saturday, the day of the game, for a tryout.

Half of Factoryville turned out for the trial,

and for two hours Christy pitched to the best hitters in the town, while the critics and judges watched. When at last he struck out the captain of the team, putting everything he had on the ball, the captain slapped him on the back and said, "You'll do. We want you to pitch this afternoon."

Christy Mathewson later called that the proudest day of his life. Arm-weary from the long tryout, he climbed into the three-bench wagon and sat beside the captain as a pair of horses pulled the team to the ball field 10 miles away, past all the other boys standing and watching and calling out words of encouragement to their pal "Husk," as he was then called.

Did Husk win the big game? He certainly did, by the score of 19–17. And despite his awkward crosshand grip on the bat, he caught hold of a pitch with the bases loaded, knocking it over the left fielder's head to drive in the winning runs.

At the time, Christy's heroes were the men on the town baseball team, many of whom sported mustaches and beards. They represented the pride of Factoryville on the playing fields against teams from nearby towns. Just as 4-year-old Christy had once wanted to play with the "big" boys, he now wanted to play with these men. And as before, this dream, too, came true.

Husk Mathewson became Factoryville's regular pitcher after that winning debut. When the town team disbanded in midseason, the captain of the team from Mill City, a much smaller hamlet five miles away, offered Christy a dollar a game to pitch every Saturday. Although he usually had to walk the five miles to the game and home again, the dollar in his pocket eased the weariness in his legs.

FROM BUCKNELL TO THE BIG LEAGUES

Soon after he graduated from Keystone Academy in June 1898, Christy took the train to Scranton to watch the YMCA team play the Pittston Reds. It cost him 35 cents for a ticket and a bag of peanuts. Scranton was almost a big-league team in his eyes, just a step below John McGraw's scrappy Baltimore Orioles, the National League team for whom Christy rooted.

The starting time for the game came and went, and the players continued to warm up. The crowd stirred impatiently. Suddenly, Christy felt a tap on his shoulder and heard the words, "The Scranton manager wants to see you." He dropped the bag of peanuts and followed the speaker to the field. There, the manager looked him over and said, "Our regular pitcher hasn't showed up. Would you like to pitch for us this afternoon?"

"It was like a bomb," Matty recalled. "For a moment I was staggered, and all I could do was stutter, 'Yes.'"

Mathewson (sitting center, second from left) in the first year he played with the Honesdale Eagles.

21

Mathewson (second from right, back row) was one of the greatest college athletes of his day. Writer Walter Camp, who annually picked the 11 all-American football players, added a 12th name for 1898, 1899, and 1900—Christy Mathewson.

A makeshift, oversized uniform was hastily rounded up for Christy. Everybody laughed when they saw him—but not for long. It was soon clear that the strangely dressed newcomer meant business as he struck out 13 men and won the game. After that, Mathewson pitched a few more times for Scranton. In July, however, the manager of a team in Honesdale, a coal-mining town 30 miles from home, offered him $25 a month plus room and board at the local hotel. Christy

thought it sounded like a good deal. Because he intended to begin college in the fall, the money would be most welcome.

In his debut on July 18, Mathewson defeated Goshen, 16–7. The next time out, he pitched a shutout—a rare feat in those days, when most teams made five or six errors in every game. And on July 27 he pitched an even rarer no-hitter.

That fall, Christy headed off to college. Having played high school football and basketball as well as baseball, he had been invited to attend the University of Pennsylvania. But Christy chose Bucknell, a much smaller school about 60 miles from home.

His freshman class in 1898 was the largest in the school's history. It had 75 students. Because some of these were girls, the available manpower to field a football team was not very deep. Bigger schools looked forward to playing Bucknell as a breather, a soft spot on their schedules. The Bucknell team often got clobbered by scores like 70–0. College football was still a new game and very different from today's sport. There were no forward passes, and there was plenty of hard hitting. With only one referee, brutal physical contacts and injuries tended to multiply, until the game could fairly be described as "11 prize-fights going on at the same time." Once a player was taken out of the game, he could not go back in, so the boys took the battering until they had to be carried off the field.

Christy was the fullback and kicker. He practiced the new dropkick and became one of the best at it in the country. For a dropkick, the kicker holds the ball, drops it, then kicks it just as it bounces off the ground. A dropkick field goal was worth 5 points.

Christy's dropkicks beat Army one year and gave Bucknell the first points it ever managed to score against Pennsylvania. In 1899, a new coach offered a raincoat to the first Bucknell player who could score against Penn, and a pair of shoes to the second player to do so. Christy's two dropkicks in a 20–10 loss won him both prizes.

Despite his later success in baseball, football remained his favorite sport. And even today, at schools such as Yale, Penn State, and Army, the name Mathewson is more likely to evoke memories of a football star than an ace pitcher.

Christy's college activities went beyond the athletic field. He was quiet and shy, and he often said he would give anything if he had the gift of gab and could socialize more easily. But his reserved manner did not keep him from being elected president of his junior class. He found time to play the bass horn in the band, join the glee club and the literary society, and be active in the chess and checkers clubs. His memory was so sharp that he could play seven or eight games of chess at the same time, even blindfolded, and win them all.

After his first year at Bucknell, Christy again played for Honesdale. There he met a left-handed pitcher, Dave Williams, who fooled around with what he called a "freak ball." When a lefty throws a curve, it breaks in toward a right-handed hitter. The freak pitch, however, broke away from the righthanders. Williams never used it in a game because he did not have enough control to get it over the plate. But Christy saw its possibilities. If he could master this pitch, it would give him a big weapon against right-handed batters. That, plus his fastball and drop and sweeping roundhouse curve, would make him tough to beat. And so he was.

Matty's success at Honesdale soon aroused the interest of several minor-league clubs. In July, the manager of the Taunton, Massachusetts, team in the New England League offered him $90 a month, and Matty jumped at the chance. Before reporting to the team, he stopped off in Boston and saw his first big-league game ever. As he watched future Hall of Famers Cy

Christy Mathewson, in a photo taken the day he joined the Norfolk team.

Young and Kid Nichols in action, he did not imagine that in less than two years he would be on the same field pitching against Nichols.

In his first game with Taunton, however, Christy discovered that he still had a lot to learn. Opposing batters were hitting him hard to all parts of the field, and he had no idea why. It wasn't until the game was almost over that Christy realized his catcher was tipping off the hitters to what the pitch was going to be. It turned out that the catcher was an old pal of Taunton's veteran pitcher and did not want to see his friend lose his job to Mathewson.

Matty learned another lesson at Taunton: $25 a month in cash was worth more than $90 in promises. Christy and his teammates were seldom paid, and what they did get went to the landlady to pay for their rooms. When the team went out of business in August, the players decided to play a Labor Day doubleheader and divide the gate receipts to pay their way home.

Mathewson left the New England League with a 5–2 record—and one important contact. Portland manager John Smith admired Christy's pitching, even though Smith's team had once trounced him, 19–11. In September, the Bucknell football team went to Philadelphia to play Penn. Smith, who was going to manage Norfolk in the Virginia League in 1900, was there, too. Before the game he visited Mathewson at the hotel and signed him up for $80 a month—after first assuring Christy that he would be paid regularly. That was the day Christy scored 10 points in a 20–10 loss. Smith was so impressed he immediately raised Mathewson's salary to $90.

Matty was a nervous 19 year old when he started the opening game for Norfolk in the spring of 1900. He walked the first three batters, then gave up a triple to the fourth. Before the inning ended, five runs had crossed the plate. But Christy finally settled down, and Norfolk won, 6–5.

By the middle of July, half the teams in the league had folded. Christy had already won 20 games, including a no-hitter, while losing only 2. The Philadelphia Phillies and New York Giants both wanted him, and the Norfolk owner let Christy choose which team he wanted to play for. At that time, the Phillies had a strong team and the Giants did not. Christy was tempted to go to Philadelphia because it was closer to home. But after studying both clubs' pitching staffs, he thought there would be more opportunity for him in New York.

Later in July, he reported to Giants manager George Davis. Christy's salary was $200 a month. If he made good by the end of the season, the Giants would pay Norfolk $2,000 for his contract. If he failed, they would send him back.

BIG 6

In a scene reminiscent of the day 14-year-old Christy Mathewson tried out for the Factoryville team in the middle of Main Street, Matty described his tryout in New York at 19: "The manager, George Davis, said to me, 'I want you to get out there and show what you have that makes you think you are a pitcher.'

"Davis stood at the bat himself. I shot one over, my fast one, and I had a lot of speed in those days.

"'That's a pretty good fast one you've got,' said Davis. 'Now let's have a look at your curve.'

"I pushed over that old roundhouse curve of mine which had been standing them on their heads in the minor leagues. You could see the ball beginning to break from the time it left my hand, and Davis just set himself for it, got a

---

The Polo Grounds was home to the Giants for 67 years until the team moved to San Francisco after the 1957 season. This photo, taken around 1900, shows the old wooden stadium. In 1911, a nearby railroad watchman noticed flames coming from the park, but by the time the alarm was sounded, the entire structure had burned down. A concrete stadium replaced it.

toehold on it and let go. The ball sailed far beyond the outfielders.

"'Put that one in cold storage,' said Davis. 'It's no good in this set. Now let's see what else you carry.'

"I said to him, 'I've got a drop ball I don't like much.'

"'Well, let's have a look at it,' he returned. I threw my drop ball and it broke pretty well for me.

"'Now that is what we call a curve in this league,' he said. 'Practice on that one. Got anything else?'

"'Sort of a freak ball,' I answered. 'It's a slow one that breaks toward a right-handed hitter.'

"'Pass it up here,' he ordered.

"I slipped him the freak pitch. Although I could not control it very well at the time, this one broke very nicely, and Davis made a vicious lunge, missing it by about two feet. We tried it again and again he missed, though this time he was looking for it.

"'That's a change of pace with a curveball,' he commented, 'a slow inshoot to a right-handed batter. It starts coming in, then sort of fades away. I never saw that before. It's all right.'

"He summoned some left-handed batters to get a line on its effectiveness against them and nearly all of them missed it."

And so Christy's freak pitch became known as the "fadeaway." Mathewson would have been a top pitcher without it, for he had everything else it takes. But that pitch, which is now called a screwball, made him even better.

It would be grand to tell how Matty broke into the big leagues with a bang, but the fact is he got his ears pinned back in his very first appearance as a Giant. Davis called for him in the 5th inning of a tie game at Brooklyn with two men on base. Christy quickly broke the tie—hitting three batters, walking another two, and giving up six runs in a 13–7 loss. Nevertheless, the newspapers generously reported that, "Matty has lots of speed and gives promise of making his way."

The Giants management was less impressed, though. After Matty lost his next three games, the Giants returned him to Norfolk without paying for him. That winter, Connie Mack offered Christy a $1,200 contract to pitch for the new Philadelphia team in the American League,

The young Mathewson won 20 games in 1901, his first full season with the Giants. Though the Rookie of the Year Award was not instituted until 1948, Mathewson was retroactively named the National League winner in a poll of the Society for American Baseball Research (SABR) members in 1987.

which had just been founded. Matty agreed and accepted $50 in advance. Meanwhile, the Cincinnati team claimed Matty from Norfolk for $100, which they were allowed to do under the rules, and immediately traded him back to the Giants. It looked as if a sneaky deal had been made to enable the Giants to keep Matty without paying Norfolk the agreed upon $2,000. But Christy did not know anything about that. As far as he was concerned, the Giants had given up on him, and now they were threatening to get the law after him if he signed with Philadelphia.

The Giants warned Christy that the new American League would not last three months. At that time, they predicted, he would be out of a job and out of baseball for good, because the National League would not let him play again. Christy did not know what to do. He had given his word to Connie Mack and had taken money in advance, but he did not want to see his prospects go up in smoke if the new league failed. So when the Giants assured him they would repay the $50 to Mack, he signed another contract with them—this time for $1,500.

Connie Mack threatened to take Christy to court, but he never did. Philadelphia fans accused Mathewson of going back on his word, booing the Bucknell football hero when he and the Giants came to town early in 1901.

It took a while for that season to get started, as rain delayed play for six days. When the sun finally came out, Christy pitched the Giants to a 5–3 win over the Dodgers. On May 6, he won his fourth straight, blanking the Phillies, 4–0, and the big city's hero worship began.

Matty gave the fans plenty to cheer about in 1901. He won his first eight games, with four shutouts, before losing, 1–0, to St. Louis on May 28. On July 15, he pitched a no-hitter against the Cardinals. The Giants had a weak team and finished seventh, but Matty wound up with a 20–17 record, finishing 36 of the 38 games he started.

As the season went on, Matty's place in the hearts of fans everywhere grew larger. This was a time when most players were rough, uneducated fellows, known for their brawling, gambling, and swearing. And the fans were often just as unruly; they took delight in hurling bottles and rotten eggs at visiting players as well as at any umpire brave—or foolish—enough to call a close one against the home team.

Then along came Matty, a college man, calm, dignified, standing tall above the rowdy crowd. His conduct commanded respect. His clean-cut, handsome features helped, too. Matty's very presence improved the game's image. The National League had been weakened when the upstart American League signed some of its best players and began luring its fans away, too. But Matty drew big crowds wherever he pitched.

It was about this time that the nickname "Big 6" was pinned on Mathewson. When Matty first showed up at the Polo Grounds, somebody said, "Here comes another six-footer." Another player took one look at Matty, who stood almost 6 feet 2 inches and appeared even taller, and said, "That's the biggest six-footer you ever saw."

In any case, the nickname caught on. Years later, a man in Chicago cut a big number 6 out of a newspaper headline, pasted it on an envelope, and mailed it. The letter was delivered directly to Matty in Los Angeles. Long a big man in New York, he had become a true national hero.

5
MATTY MEETS MCGRAW

As a rookie, Christy Mathewson would put everything he had on every pitch. One day, he got tired and lost a game by giving up four runs in the 9th inning. Afterward, George Davis gave him some valuable advice: "Don't pitch your head off when you don't need to."

Nobody ever had to tell Christy Mathewson something more than once. From then on, he did not go for the strikeout unless he was in a tight spot. Instead, he invited the batter to hit the ball, conserving his strength and his best stuff for the pinch. In this way he got through many games throwing fewer than 100 pitches, once completing a game with only 67. He made batters hit the ball *he* wanted them to hit. With his excellent memory, he knew what kind of ball every batter liked and did not like.

One day, a young player got three hits off Christy and boasted, "So that's the great Mathewson?"

Mathewson, a devoted family man, watches as his son, Christopher, Jr., shows his pitching motion.

"Do you know what kind of pitches they were that you hit?" asked an older player.

"No," the youngster said carelessly. "Who cares?"

"Well, Matty does," the veteran said, "and you can bet you'll never get any of those pitches from him again."

Mathewson never stopped practicing his control, and he soon developed the ability to throw the ball exactly where he wanted it to go. He once worked 68 innings without giving up a walk, and he averaged a remarkable 1.59 walks for each 9 innings he pitched over a 17-year period.

Nobody described the way Matty could pitch better than Ring Lardner, a Chicago sportswriter who used a typical 1901 fan's dialect to do it: "I bet he could shave you if he wanted to and if he had a razor blade to throw instead of a ball. If you can't hit a fast one a inch and a quarter inside and he knows it, you'll get three fast ones a inch and a quarter inside and then, if you've swung at 'em you can go and get a drink of water."

Matty started his second season with two new suits—tokens of appreciation from the club's owner—and a raise to $3,000. The Giants were a raggedy last-place team in 1902, however. Although he pitched eight shutouts, Matty lost more games than he won. Still, it turned out to be the turning point of his career, because that summer John McGraw left Baltimore and took over as the Giants' manager.

Most fans and experts figured Christy Mathewson and John McGraw would go together like ketchup on corn flakes. McGraw was known as a man who would do anything he could get away with to win. He was always beefing at

*"The Little Napoleon,"
manager John McGraw,
flanked by his two pitching
aces, Mathewson (left) and
"Iron Man" Joe McGinnity.*

umpires, and he got into more fights than a
sackful of cats and dogs. To top it all off, he used
the kind of language that would make the folks
in Factoryville close the shutters and cover their
ears. When a player made a foolish mistake,
McGraw would tongue-lash him unmercifully.

But as tough as he was, McGraw was a fair
man. He treated everyone the same. McGraw
was especially impressed with Mathewson's intelligence. He firmly believed that in baseball,
brains counted for more than brawn, and Matty
clearly knew how to use his head. With McGraw
as his teacher, Christy became a dedicated student of the science of pitching. He practiced long
hours without being pushed, and accepted discipline cheerfully. He quickly became McGraw's
model of a perfect pitching machine.

Manager and pitcher got along so well that when Matty married a former Bucknell student named Jane Stoughton in 1903, the young couple shared an apartment in New York with Mr. and Mrs. McGraw for a while. The two women remained lifelong friends.

From Baltimore, McGraw brought veteran pitcher "Iron Man" Joe McGinnity and catcher Roger Bresnahan to New York. McGinnity earned his nickname by more than once pitching—and winning—both games of a doubleheader. Bresnahan was a fiery Irishman like McGraw, with a memory as keen as Matty's. Once he discovered a weak spot in the opposition, he never forgot it.

With McGinnity winning 31 and Matty 30, the Giants shot up to second place in 1903, and

Jane Mathewson with her son, Christopher, Jr. in a photo taken about 1912. The young Mathewson was not a major league pitcher like his father and uncle, but he became a fighter pilot in World War II.

they ran away with the pennant in each of the next two years. Matty won 33 in 1904 and 31 in 1905.

The 1905 Giants were pure McGraw: a smart, quick-thinking team of fighters who believed they could beat anybody, anytime. Matty pitched his second no-hitter on June 13, edging Mordecai "Three Finger" Brown of the Cubs, 1–0. Though he and Brown would tangle in many big games over the years (with Brown winning most of them), Mathewson enjoyed the challenge of pitting his skills against the Cub ace.

The first World Series had been played in 1903. The rivalry between leagues was so fierce that the Giants actually refused to play the American League winner in 1904. But with peace declared between the two leagues, they went into the 1905 Series against the team that had signed Christy Mathewson before he jumped back to the Giants—Connie Mack's Philadelphia Athletics.

The Philadelphia fans had never really forgiven Matty, but by the time the Series was over they could not help but admire and respect him. Mathewson shut them out three times in six days, something no other pitcher has ever done. Altogether, the Athletics managed only 14 hits in those three games, as Matty struck out 18 batters and walked just one. And then McGinnity stepped in, winning the fourth for New York with still another shutout.

John McGraw had so much confidence in Mathewson that he never once took him out of a game. Instead, he left it to Matty to decide whether or not he had the stuff to continue. If he had a big lead, Matty never cared how many hits or runs the other team made—as long as they did

not catch up. Sometimes, this made McGraw nervous, and then Matty would obligingly strike out the side to calm him.

Of course, Matty was not a machine, and he occasionally had his off days. Once, in 1906, he was unable to get anybody out. The Cubs pounded him and two other Giants pitchers for a 19–0 shellacking.

On another day, Matty was warming up before a crucial game. McGraw stood alongside him, smiling in approval as the fastballs thumped into the catcher's mitt and the curves snapped off sharply. But after a lengthy warm-up, Christy turned to McGraw and silently shook his head. McGraw called for another pitcher to warm up, and then he went back to the bench.

"Matty's not ready today," he told the other players. "There's a man who has the courage to say 'No' and to stop rather than try to be a hero. Matty used his head instead of his heart."

Mathewson was a brainy player at a time when a premium was placed on the ability to outwit and outthink the other team, rather than the ability to hit the ball out of the park. But he was not immune from superstition. One day,

This rare action sequence shows Christy Mathewson in his pitching motion. According to baseball historian Fred Lieb, Mathewson's fastball was below that of Nolan Ryan, Bob Feller, Lefty Grove, and Walter Johnson, but his motion was so smooth that his pitch was often in on hitters before they realized it.

while he was walking in New York with a long-time friend, a minister, they passed a cross-eyed man.

Matty took off his new hat and spat in it.

"What's the matter with you?" the surprised preacher asked.

"Spit in your hat quick and kill the jinx," Matty answered.

The preacher whipped off his silk top hat and did as he was told.

"What's the idea?" he asked.

"Worst jinx in the world to see a cross-eyed man," Christy said. "But I hope it didn't hurt your silk hat."

"Not at all," said his good natured friend. "But I'm glad the percentage of cross-eyed men is small."

Some players believed that finding hairpins or seeing a wagonload of empty barrels meant sure base hits, while crossed bats lying on the ground would lead to a bad day at the plate. And Matty once announced that he would rather freeze to death than warm up with a third baseman.

6

THE MOST FAMOUS BASEBALL GAME EVER PLAYED

Detroit Tigers star Ty Cobb and Mathewson talk before Matty took the mound for game 3 of the 1911 World Series. Mathewson is wearing the black Giants uniform that manager McGraw first unveiled in the 1905 World Series against the Athletics.

In 1908, Christy Mathewson pitched the biggest game of his life—and lost it. To make matters worse, it was a game the Giants believed they should never have been forced to play.

While the Cubs were going for their third straight pennant, the Giants and Pirates battled them down to the last day of the season. There have been more words written about the game between the Giants and Cubs on September 23, 1908, than any other game in the history of baseball. But few people know that Matty's honesty was responsible for his team's defeat that day. This is what happened:

The score was tied, 1–1, in the bottom of the 9th, and the Giants had men on first and third with 2 out. When the next batter singled, the winning run appeared to score. In the excitement, however, the man on first, a rookie named Fred Merkle, turned and headed for the clubhouse without going all the way to touch second base. Players often did that in similar situations. Matty, who had pitched the game and was coaching at first base at the time, joyfully followed Merkle as the fans ran onto the field. But a Cub infielder somehow got hold of the ball and touched second base. He then announced that Merkle was out on a force-out and the run did not count. The umpires agreed. By this time the Giants were already in the showers and the field was filled with people, so the game could not be continued. It was called a tie.

The Giants protested to the league directors, claiming the victory. Some New York players swore that Merkle had really touched second base; others declared they had thrown the ball into the grandstand and therefore the Cubs could not have picked it up and held it at second base. It was a bitter argument, full of conflicting stories.

The league directors were about to decide in favor of the Giants when they came upon a statement written by Mathewson, which they had originally overlooked. Matty's honesty was beyond question. Sometimes, when there was only one umpire in a game and his view of the play was blocked, the ump would actually ask Mathewson for help in calling the play, with complete confidence that Matty would call it as he saw it—even if it went against his own team. So when they discovered his statement, the directors were prepared to base their decision on it. Matty knew that Merkle had not touched second base, and that is exactly what he said. The game was officially declared a tie. As a result, when the season ended, the Cubs and Giants were deadlocked, and a playoff was required.

Many of the Giants felt they had been cheated out of a pennant they had won on the field, and they did not think they should have to win it again. John McGraw left it up to them. Mathewson and four others went to see club president John T. Brush, who was sick in bed at the time.

"A lot of the boys do not believe we ought to be forced to play over again for something we have already won," Matty told him. Then, as Mathewson later recalled the rest of that meeting: "Mr. Brush looked surprised. I was nervous, more so than when I am in the box with three on the bases and [Cub slugger] Joe Tinker at bat.... We five big athletes were embarrassed in the presence of this sick man. Suddenly it struck us all at the same time that the game would have to be played to keep ourselves square with our own ideas of courage.... We all saw that, and it was this thin, ill man in bed who made us see it even before he had said a word. It was the expression on his face. It seemed to say, 'And I had confidence in you, boys, to do the right thing.' "

Fred Merkle played in five World Series for three National League teams, but he will always be remembered for his so-called "bonehead" play on September 23, 1908, the first game he ever started. As the runner on first, he failed to touch second base after the batter drove home what would have been the winning run from third. The opposing team made a force-out on Merkle.

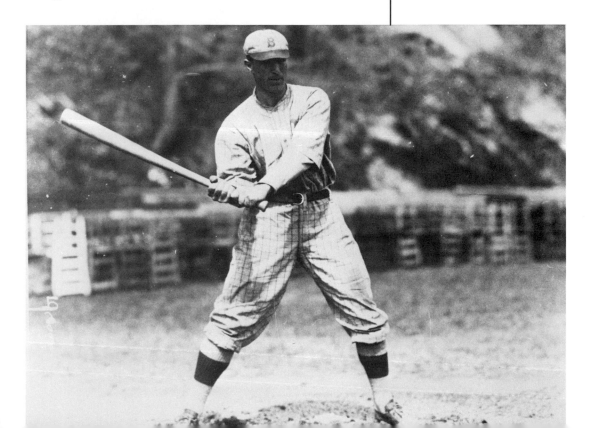

The night before the playoff game, a noisy crowd gathered outside the Polo Grounds. When the gates opened, the seats were quickly filled to overflowing. In fact, the police needed fire hoses to keep the fans from tearing down the fences to get inside. Fights broke out everywhere, even on the field, where some players started mixing it up before the game.

This was the one game Mathewson wanted to win more than any other, but when he woke up that morning he did not think he had it in him. He had already won 37 games that year, including 12 shutouts, pitching a grand total of 391 innings. When his wife asked him at breakfast if he was going to pitch that day, he said, "No. My arm is heavy as a board."

But there was no way John McGraw was going to entrust this game to anyone but his best pitcher, no matter how bad Matty's arm felt.

The Giants took a 1–0 lead in the opening inning against Cubs starter Jack Pfeister. But then the Cubs brought in Three Finger Brown, who had beaten Matty in every one of their last eight meetings. This time, Matty had nothing but grit; his curve just was not breaking. Joe Tinker hit a triple in the 3rd inning. Matty looked toward the bench, but McGraw signaled him to stay out there. A walk and three more hits brought in four runs and finished the Giants. The final score: 4–2.

It took the Giants three more years to beat out the Cubs and begin their own three-year reign as National League champions. But they could not win a single World Series. The Philadelphia Athletics defeated them twice, in 1911 and 1913. And in 1912, a string of bad breaks snatched the final-game victory from Christy's

"Mathewson wasn't a kid any longer by the time we got into the '12 Series," Red Sox pitcher Smokey Joe Wood later related to writer Don Honig. "I don't think he was as fast as he'd once been. When I saw him his greatest asset was control and a beautiful curveball. He'd also threw what they called a fadeaway, which is the same as a screwball. As far as I knew, he was the only one who threw it at the time."

grasp as the Giants bowed to the Boston Red Sox.

Christy Mathewson not only played in the 1912 Series; he actually covered it as a special reporter for a New York newspaper. As things turned out, Matty had his problems with both jobs. In the process, however, he provided the fans with an immortal nickname. It all began when Frank Baker hit a home run off Giants lefty Rube Marquard to win the second game. Matty wrote that Marquard had not pitched correctly to Baker. Then, in the very next game, the Giants were ahead 1–0 in the 9th when Baker came to bat. This time Baker hit a home run off

Mathewson wearing makeup for The Umpire, *one of the early silent movies in which he appeared.*

Mathewson to tie the score, and the A's went on to win. Marquard, who was writing his own stories for another paper, wrote that Matty sure knew what he was talking about, because he had made the same mistake. From then on, Baker was known as Home Run Baker.

By 1912, Mathewson was one of the highest paid players, earning $10,000 a year. In his spare time, he wrote magazine articles, plays, and books. He also starred in a few silent movies and was in great demand on the vaudeville circuit, teaming up with three other players in a singing quartet and a baseball skit. Thanks to some sound investments in the stock market, his financial future seemed secure. Still, when a new major league, the Federal League, offered him a three-year contract for $65,000 in 1914, Matty was flattered. That was more money than any player had ever seen. It was more, he thought, than any player was worth.

Recalling the big $90-a-month contract he had signed for in the short-lived New England League, Matty was leery of the new league's chances of success. He did not criticize lesser-paid players for jumping at the offers, but he felt he had been treated well by the Giants and did not think it would be right to desert them.

Wh en a team trades a player who has been its greatest and most popular star for 16 years, it may seem like a coldhearted, even cruel, thing to do. But when John McGraw traded Christy Mathewson along with outfielder Edd Roush and infielder Bill McKechnie to the Cincinnati Reds in July 1916, he was actually doing Big 6 a favor. Matty, who was then almost 36, wanted to stay in baseball even after he could no longer win on the mound, and he was going to the Reds with the understanding that he would be the team's manager.

Roush and McKechnie were not sorry about the trade either—but for different reasons. As they sat on the train to Cincinnati, they talked about how happy they were to be leaving New York. Mathewson listened in silence to their complaints about the Giants manager.

John McGraw with his coach, Christy Mathewson. Mathewson said of the manager, "I have seen McGraw go onto ball fields where he is as welcome as a man with the black small pox...I have seen him take all sorts of personal chances. He doesn't know what fear is."

After a while, Roush turned to him and said, "Well, Matty, aren't you glad to be getting away from McGraw?"

Mathewson shook his head. "I appreciate McGraw making a place for me in baseball and giving me this managing job. He's doing me a favor, and I thanked him for it."

The game of baseball was changing, the long ball becoming more prominent. Matty's style had always been to make as few throws in a game as he could get away with, tempting batters to hit the first pitch. He could still finish a game on 70 or 80 pitches in an hour and a half. But that style had become more dangerous as the home run became more common. In 1914, despite an impressive 24–13 record, Mathewson allowed 16 home runs—more than any other pitcher had given up in the previous five years. An arm injury and his advancing years accounted for Matty's 8–4 record in 1915. And he was 3–4 for the Giants when the trade was made.

For sentimental reasons—and to draw a crowd—the Reds' new manager pitched one game for Cincinnati against none other than Three Finger Brown on September 4, 1916. Matty won it, 10–8, giving him 373 wins, a National League record he still shares with Grover Cleveland Alexander.

John McGraw and Christy Mathewson had long shared the adoration of New Yorkers. When Matty returned to the Polo Grounds in a Reds uniform, the fans were not quite sure who to root for. They settled the problem by yelling and cheering for Matty, and then bellowing just as enthusiastically for McGraw. Reporters noted that when the game was over, Matty had gotten the greater share of the cheers.

The Reds finished the 1916 season tied for last place, then climbed to fourth in 1917 and third in 1918. As a pitcher, he had always inspired confidence in the other players. His teammates loved him and did their best to win for him. As manager, he earned the same respect and devotion from his players.

But there were bigger issues than the National League pennant that would affect Mathewson. World War I had been raging in Europe since 1914, and the United States entered the war in 1917. As the conflict continued into 1918, Mathewson left the Reds with just 10 games remaining in the season and accepted a commission as a captain in the Chemical Warfare (better known as the Gas and Flame) Division. The Germans had been spraying poison gas on the soldiers in the trenches, and many had died from its effects. It was Matty's job to teach young recruits how to protect themselves from such attacks.

On the troopship going to France, Captain Mathewson caught the flu. It was a cold, damp autumn, and he could not shake off the effects of the illness. As part of their training, the troops would go into a building where lethal mustard gas was injected into the air. Time and again Matty went in with them to demonstrate the correct way of putting on a gas mask. Already weakened by the flu, his lungs took in a dangerous amount of gas fumes.

After the war ended in November 1918, the Cincinnati Reds wanted him to return as manager for the 1919 season. But he was out in the trenches somewhere in Europe, and the telegram they sent never reached him. Pat Moran was given the job and led the Reds to the NL pennant.

Mathewson poses proudly in his uniform after quitting the Reds and enlisting in the army in 1918.

8

MATTY'S LAST GAME

Gilbert Mathewson, 77, sits with his son Christy at a Boston Braves game in 1924. Before the game, Mathewson, the president of the Braves, watched his father march around the field with other veterans of the Civil War.

When Matty finally came home that spring, John McGraw gave him a coaching job with the Giants. In the fall, he wrote all about the World Series between the Reds and the Chicago White Sox for a New York newspaper. He was one of the first to report that the games were not on the up-and-up. It was later confirmed that several Chicago players had been bribed to throw the Series.

Throughout the 1919 season, Mathewson suffered from a chronic cough. At first, the doctors said it was bronchitis, but it turned out to be something much more serious. In 1920, Matty went to a sanitarium in Saranac Lake, New York, and began the biggest battle of his life—against the disease of tuberculosis.

Christy Mathewson was in for a long stay at Saranac Lake. He and his wife built a small house there. In the nearby fields, Matty learned to identify hundreds of wildflowers. He played checkers and bridge when the doctors allowed. But mostly he had to rest.

Of course, there was still baseball. No matter

Christy Mathewson's 1911 baseball card.

how sick he felt, Matty followed the Giants closely. And when the team stormed from behind to clinch the 1921 pennant against the Pirates, John McGraw called him from Pittsburgh. McGraw's hotel room was filled with reporters, and Matty asked to say a few words to each of them. The tough baseball manager and the cynical newspapermen had a hard time blinking back their tears as they wished Mathewson luck in the fight to regain his health.

At the end of the season, the Giants organized Christy Mathewson Day, the receipts to go to the Old Master of the Mound. A ball autographed by President Warren Harding, Vice-President Calvin Coolidge, Babe Ruth, Giants first baseman George Kelly, and Mathewson himself was auctioned for $750. Altogether, more than $40,000 was raised.

By 1923, Matty felt sure he was cured, and he accepted the position of president of the Boston Braves. While everyone in the game cheered his return, his wife was fearful—and with good reason. The work proved too much for him. In the spring of 1925, Christy Mathewson had a relapse and returned to Saranac Lake.

On October 7 of that year, Walter Johnson, Matty's American League rival for the title of world's greatest pitcher, defeated the Pittsburgh Pirates in game 1 of the World Series. But the thoughts of many old-timers watching that game were with another great hurler.

As 37-year-old Johnson pitched in his last World Series, 45-year-old Mathewson lay in great pain. He called in his wife, who had long been his nurse and loving companion. Gathering all his remaining strength, he sat up in bed and asked for a pencil and paper. "It is no use," he said. "I am going to die and we must face it." Then he calmly told her how to arrange his last journey home, writing down the departure times of the trains plus a few final instructions. Then he added, "Now I suppose you will have to have a good cry. But don't make it a long one. It cannot be helped."

When Jane Mathewson returned to the sickroom that night, her husband was barely alive. Still, he managed a courageous smile. "Are you sure you are all right, Janie, dear?" he said very faintly. And a short while later, he sank back gently on his bed and died. Christy Mathewson was buried in a little cemetery near the Bucknell campus, where he had been a hero. To honor him, both World Series teams wore black armbands for the rest of the games.

The day after Matty's death, New York sports editor W. O. McGeehan wrote: "While the captains and the kings of baseball were gathered here last night after the first game of the World Series, there died at Saranac the best loved of all baseball players and the most popular of all American athletes of all times—Christy Mathewson.

"If baseball will hold the ideals and the example of Christy Mathewson, gentleman, sportsman, and soldier, our national game will keep the younger generation clean and courageous and the future of the nation secure."

When the Baseball Hall of Fame was created in 1936, Christy Mathewson was one of the first men to be inducted. And when Jane Mathewson died in 1967, she left her husband's baseball mementos to the Keystone Academy, near Factoryville, where they can be seen today to keep alive the memory of Christy Mathewson, one of America's greatest baseball heroes.

CHRONOLOGY

Aug. 12, 1880	Born in Factoryville, Pennsylvania.
1899	Signs first minor league contract with Taunton in the New England League.
July 17, 1900	Makes major league debut with New York Giants.
July 15, 1901	Pitches first no-hitter, 5–0, against St. Louis Cardinals.
1903	Marries Jane Stoughton.
June 13, 1905	Pitches second no-hitter, 1–0, versus Cubs.
1905	Pitches three shutouts in six days in World Series against Philadelphia Athletics.
1908	Wins N. L. record 37 games.
Sept. 15, 1908	Beats Cardinals for 24th straight time, a major league record.
1913	Sets record giving up fewest walks per game—.62 —and pitches a record 68 innings without walking a batter; pitches 4th shutout and 10th complete game in World Series play.
July 20, 1916	Is traded to Cincinnati Reds and named manager.
Sept. 4, 1916	Beats Cubs, 10–8, for 373rd and final victory.
1918	Enlists in U.S. Army as captain in Chemical Warfare Division.
1921	Enters sanitarium for treatment of tuberculosis.
1923	Returns as president of the Boston Braves.
Oct. 7, 1925	Dies at Saranac Lake, New York.

CHRISTY MATHEWSON
NEW YORK, N.L., 1900-1916.
CINCINNATI, N.L., 1916.
BORN FACTORYVILLE, PA., AUGUST 12, 1880
GREATEST OF ALL THE GREAT PITCHERS
IN THE 20TH CENTURY'S FIRST QUARTER
PITCHED 3 SHUTOUTS IN 1905 WORLD SERIES.
FIRST PITCHER OF THE CENTURY EVER TO
WIN 30 GAMES IN 3 SUCCESSIVE YEARS.
WON 37 GAMES IN 1908
"MATTY WAS MASTER OF THEM ALL"

MAJOR LEAGUE STATISTICS

NEW YORK GIANTS, CINCINNATI REDS

YEAR	TEAM	W	L	PCT	ERA	G	GS	CG	IP	H	BB	SO	ShO
1900	NY N	0	3	.000	4.76	5	1	1	34	35	14	15	0
1901		20	17	.541	2.41	40	38	36	336	288	97	221	5
1902		14	17	.452	2.11	34	32	29	276.2	241	73	159	8
1903		30	13	.698	2.26	45	42	37	366.1	321	100	267	3
1904		33	12	.733	2.03	48	46	33	367.2	306	78	212	4
1905		31	8	.795	1.27	43	37	33	339	252	64	206	8
1906		22	12	.647	2.97	38	35	22	266.2	262	77	128	6
1907		24	13	.649	1.99	41	36	31	316	250	53	178	8
1908		37	11	.771	1.43	56	44	34	390.2	285	42	259	12
1909		25	6	.806	1.14	37	33	26	275.1	192	36	149	8
1910		27	9	.750	1.90	38	35	27	318	292	60	184	2
1911		26	13	.667	1.99	45	37	29	307	303	38	141	5
1912		23	12	.657	2.12	43	34	27	310	311	24	134	0
1913		25	11	.694	2.06	40	35	25	306	291	21	93	4
1914		24	13	.649	3.00	41	35	29	312	314	23	80	5
1915		8	14	.364	3.58	27	24	11	186	199	20	57	1
1916	2 teams		NY N (3–4)		Cin N (1–0)								
	total	4	4	.500	3.01	13	7	5	74.2	74	8	19	1
Totals		373	188	.665	2.13	634	551	435	4782	4216	838	2502	80
World Series (4 years)		5	5	.500	1.15	11	11	10	101.2	76	10	48	4

FURTHER READING

Alexander, Charles C. *John McGraw.* New York: Viking Penguin, 1988.

Allen, Lee. *The National League Story.* New York: Hill & Wang, 1961.

Broeg, Bob. *Super Stars of Baseball.* St. Louis: The Sporting News, 1971.

Charlton, James. *The Baseball Chronology.* New York: Macmillan, 1991.

Graham, Frank. *McGraw of the Giants.* New York: G.P. Putnam, 1944.

Graham, Frank. *The New York Giants.* New York: G.P. Putnam, 1952.

Mathewson, Christy. *Pitching in a Pinch.* New York: G.P. Putnam, 1912.

McGraw, John J. *My 30 Years in Baseball.* New York: Boni & Liveright, 1923.

Meany, Tom. *Baseball's Greatest Pitchers.* New York: A. S. Barnes, 1951.

Schoor, Gene. *Christy Mathewson, Baseball's Greatest Pitcher.* New York: Julian Messner, 1953.

Shapiro, Milton J. *Baseball's Greatest Pitchers.* New York: Julian Messner, 1969.

INDEX

Page numbers in italics refer to illustrations.

PICTURE CREDITS
Bucknell University, Lewisburg, PA: p. 23; Keystone Junior College, La Plume, PA: pp. 2, 8, 14, 16, 18, 25, 31, 34, 38, 40-41, 48,
    54; National Baseball Library, Cooperstown, NY: pp. 11, 20, 37, 42, 45, 47, 53, 58, 60; New York Historical Society: p. 28;
Ken Robbins: p. 56

NORMAN MACHT was a minor league general manager with the Milwaukee Braves and Baltimore Orioles organizations and has been a stock broker and college professor. His work has appeared in *The BallPlayers*, *The Sporting News*, *Baseball Digest* and *Sports Heritage*, and he is the co-author with Dick Bartell of *Rowdy Richard*. Norman Macht lives in Newark, Delaware.

JIM MURRAY, veteran sports columnist of the *Los Angeles Times*, is one of America's most acclaimed writers. He has been named "America's Best Sportswriter" by the National Association of Sportscasters and Sportswriters 14 times, was awarded the Red Smith Award, and was twice winner of the National Headliner Award. In addition, he was awarded the J. G. Taylor Spink Award in 1987 for "meritorious contributions to baseball writing." With this award came his 1988 induction into the National Baseball Hall of Fame in Cooperstown, New York. In 1990, Jim Murray was awarded the Pulitzer Prize for Commentary.

EARL WEAVER is the winningest manager in Baltimore Orioles history by a wide margin. He compiled 1,480 victories in his 17 years at the helm. After managing eight different minor league teams, he was given the chance to lead the Orioles in 1968. Under his leadership the Orioles finished lower than second place in the American League East only four times in 17 years. One of only 12 managers in big league history to have managed in four or more World Series, Earl was named Manager of the Year in 1979. The popular Weaver had his number 5 retired in 1982, joining Brooks Robinson, Frank Robinson, and Jim Palmer, whose numbers were retired previously. Earl Weaver continues his association with the professional baseball scene by writing, broadcasting, and coaching.